MW00762473

MONSTERS

CERBERUS

BY SHIRLEY-RAYE REDMOND

KIDHAVEN PRESS
A part of Gale, Cengage Learning

GALE
CENGAGE Learning™

Detroit • New York • San Francisco • New Haven, Conn • Waterville, Maine • London

© 2009 Gale, Cengage Learning

LIBRARY OF CONGRESS CATALOGING-IN-PUBLICATION DATA

Redmond, Shirley-Raye, 1955–
   Cerberus / by Shirley-Raye Redmond.
     p. cm. — (Monsters)
   Includes bibliographical references and index.
   ISBN 978-0-7377-4274-9 (hardcover)
   1. Cerberus (Greek mythology)—Juvenile literature. I. Title.
   BL820.C4R43 2009
   398.24'540938—dc22

                                      2008026600

KidHaven Press
27500 Drake Rd.
Farmington Hills, MI 48331

ISBN-13: 978-0-7377-4274-9
ISBN-10: 0-7377-4274-7

Contents

CHAPTER 1

DEMON FROM THE PIT

The ancient Greeks lived in Europe thousands of years ago, between 3000 B.C. and 130 B.C. They were intelligent and creative. They built beautiful theaters and temples. They had powerful armies and strong athletes. They started the first Olympic games so long ago that there is no record of the date of the first competition. The ancient Greeks also had many stories about mythical beasts and monsters. One of the most dreaded was a black, three-headed dog called Cerberus. The word comes from an ancient Greek term meaning "demon from the pit." Some say that the center head was that of a raging lion, with a thick mane of wriggling snakes. The other heads were those of a snarling dog or wolf.

4

His tail was like a dragon's tail. In some tales, Cerberus has 100 heads and in others 50.

Cerberus guarded the gates to hell. He had supernatural strength and a bloodthirsty temperament. His duty was to eat intruders who crossed the River Styx and to keep the spirits from escaping. His master was **Hades**, the unpopular, sulking god of the underworld. Hades is called Pluto in the Roman myths. He is the brother of Zeus and Poseidon (or Neptune).

Sometimes called the "hound of Hades," Cerberus was so ferocious that even his master feared him. He kept the beast chained outside the gate of his gloomy palace.

Ancient Greeks and Romans buried their dead loved ones with a coin under the tongue or two coins over the eyelids and a small honey cake. The

Cerberus was a three-headed dog who guarded the gates of the underworld in Greek mythology.

coin was payment for grim and scowling Charon, who ferried the souls across the River Styx. The cake was for Cerberus, to quiet his fierce barking. This old custom gave rise to the saying "a sop for Cerberus." It is used now to mean giving a bribe or offering a compliment or gift to quiet a troublesome customer or acquaintance.

Poisonous Dog Slobber

According to legend, Cerberus's saliva is poisonous. Wherever it drips to the ground, a poisonous plant called aconite springs up, even on bare rock and thin soil. This plant really exists and belongs to the buttercup family. Today it is commonly referred to as monkshood, devil's helmet, or wolfsbane. Perhaps it is no coincidence that for centuries, wolfsbane was thought to protect one from the bite of a werewolf. Small amounts of the dried leaves and roots were sometimes used as a **sedative** to help patients sleep. The drug slows the heart rate and decreases blood pressure. Too much is lethal and even deadly.

Doctors in ancient Greece believed that wolfsbane would neutralize the poison of scorpions and that its smell could kill rats and mice. Hecate, the Greek goddess of witchcraft, poisoned her own father with the plant. Sometimes aconite is called hecateis, after the witch. The jealous sorceress Medea in Greek mythology tried to poison the hero Theseus with this plant after he killed the

Cerberus

The flower known as wolfsbane is a poisonous plant that supposedly came from the slobber of Cerberus.

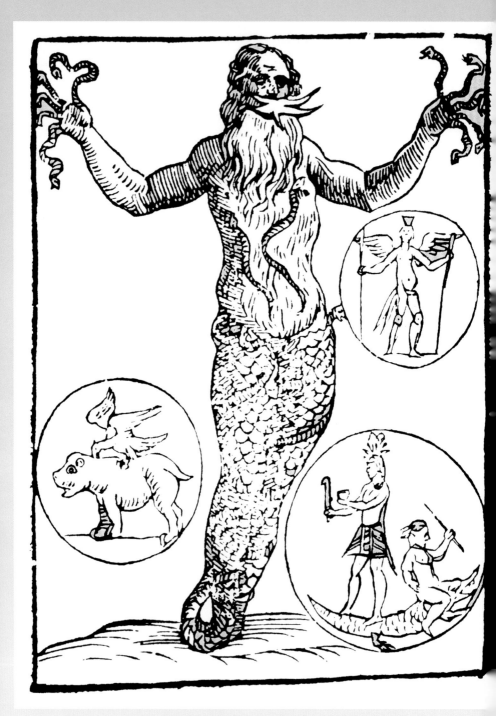

The monster Typhon was the father of Cerberus.

8   Cerberus

deadly Minotaur. In Brian Jacques's book *Outcast of Redwall,* the villainous ferret Veil poisons a resident of Redwall using wolfsbane. In the Harry Potter series, there is a foul-tasting wolfsbane potion so difficult to make that Severus Snape, the potions master and Harry Potter's least favorite teacher, is the only Hogwarts faculty member able to concoct it. He gives it to Remus Lupin, another Hogwarts teacher, when the moon is full to keep him from becoming a werewolf.

Origins

Cerberus, or Kerberos, is the horrible offspring of two dreadful monsters, Echidna and Typhon. Echidna is sometimes called the "mother of all monsters" because she gave birth to most of the monsters in Greek mythology. She was often shown with the face of a beautiful woman and the enormous, writhing body of a giant snake. Feared by both gods and **mortals**, Echidna lived in a large cave. She ate unsuspecting people who passed by the mouth of the cave, and she ate them raw.

Typhon, the storm god, was her mate. He was the fiercest of all living creatures and supposedly the largest monster who ever lived, towering above the mountain ranges. He had 100 serpent heads. Poison and flames shot from his fiercely glowing eyes. From his mouth, he spewed lava and fiery stones. He had a long, matted beard and pointed ears. More snakes sprouted from his powerful thighs. Instead of fingers, he had 100 snake heads, 50 on each gigantic fist.

Typhon and Echidna attacked the Olympian gods. The battle was fierce. Typhon tore up mountains from the earth and hurled them at Zeus, the ruler of the universe. Zeus hurled his mighty thunderbolts at raging Typhon. In the end Zeus defeated the fearsome monster couple and imprisoned them deep in the bowels of the earth. Later Argos, the giant with 100 eyes, killed Echidna while she slept. It is said, however, that Typhon still lives, trapped under the volcano Mount Etna in Sicily. Some say the flames and smoke rising from the volcano's peak are really caused by the raging monster.

Besides Cerberus, their beastly offspring included the Hydra, a water monster with nine snake heads, and the Sphinx, a winged lion with a woman's head. The Chimera was a strange creature that exhaled scorching fire. It was part lion, part goat, and part snake. The vicious Nemean Lion had tough skin that no man's weapon could pierce. Cerberus also had a **canine** brother—Orthus, a monstrous dog with two heads and a snake's tail.

A Deadly Duo

According to the earliest tales told about them, Cerberus and Orthus were vicious beasts who no mortal could slay. They had jaws of steel and a hunger for human flesh. Unstoppable forces of

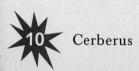

Cerberus

hellish destruction, their very names struck fear into the hearts of men. Some tales say that it was fierce Orthus, not his father Typhon, who fathered the monsters Chimera, Sphinx, and the Nemean Lion, with his own mother, Echidna.

While Cerberus guarded the gates of Hades, Orthus served as a guard dog for a fabulous herd of red-skinned cattle owned by his master, Geryon. Geryon was a hideous warrior giant with three heads and three bodies joined at the waist. Some stories say he had six legs and six arms. Others say the three upper bodies were joined at the waist to

The three-headed giant Geryon was the owner of Cerberus's brother Orthus.

one pair of legs. This giant was also king of the isle of Erythia, in the western Mediterranean. In one well-known myth, the hero Hercules was sent to the island to steal the cattle. It was a long and dangerous journey. As soon as he stepped ashore, the fierce two-headed watchdog attacked Hercules, who slew him with one mighty swing of his club. Another version of the tale says the hero strangled him with his bare hands. Hercules then killed the herdsman, Eurytion. But just as Hercules was escaping with the cattle, the enraged giant Geryon charged after him. Hercules shot him dead with a poisonous arrow.

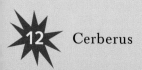

Chapter 2

Confronting the Beast

Tales of the fierce, flesh-eating monster struck fear in the heart of everyone who heard them. These fantastic tales had been passed down from one generation of Greeks and Romans to the next. There are several stories about mythical heroes confronting the ferocious watchdog. However, unlike his brother Orthus, Cerberus was never killed. The most famous heroic tale is that of Hercules. The Greeks called him Herakles.

Hercules and Cerberus

Hercules was the strongest hero in Greek and Roman mythology. He was the son of the god Zeus and a human mother named Alcmene. When

13

Hera, the wife of Zeus, drove Hercules mad, he went into a rage and accidentally killed his own children and his nephews. The gods punished him by making him perform twelve impossible tasks or labors. King Eurytheus was given the privilege of

Hercules was the only man strong enough to capture Cerberus.

 Cerberus

naming those tasks. The king saved the worst for last. He ordered Hercules to kidnap Cerberus from hell and bring him back—alive—to the palace. With the help of the god Hermes (Mercury), Hercules made the long and frightening journey to the underworld and presented himself before Hades and his queen, Persephone. He explained his reason for coming, and Hades agreed to permit him to take the black hellhound to King Eurytheus, on the condition that Hercules not kill the beast, as he had killed Orthus.

Using all of his superhuman strength, Hercules wrestled with the savage, slobbering beast. Poisonous plants sprang up everywhere that Cerberus's saliva dripped to the ground. Hercules finally subdued the hellhound. He bound him in chains and delivered him to the palace. King Eurytheus was so frightened by the snarling monster that he hid in a large storage jar so he would not have to look upon it. Later, the king had Cerberus released, and the beast returned to his watchdog duties in the underworld.

Orpheus Soothes the Savage Beast

Hercules was not the only brave hero bold enough to confront the fearsome hellhound. Orpheus, a legendary musician, risked his life to rescue his beloved bride, Eurydice, from the **netherworld**. Armed only with a stringed instrument called a **lyre**, Orpheus made his descent into the dark

caverns that smelled of sulfur, or hellfire. Along the
way he sang. According to legend he was the best
singer who ever lived. Trees bent down to listen to

*Orpheus was able to get permission to take his wife
Eurydice out of the underworld by charming Hades,
Persephone, and Cerberus with his music.*

Cerberus

him. Animals came out of their hiding places to hear his song. Orpheus's voice was so beautiful that even ferocious Cerberus—enchanted—stopped his savage barking and sat down on his massive haunches to listen. Soon he fell asleep.

Before the throne of gloomy Hades, Orpheus presented his case. He explained that a poisonous snake had bitten young Eurydice on their wedding day. Her death had been sudden and unexpected. She deserved another chance in life. Then Orpheus sang for the king of the underworld and his queen. They wept as they listened. Hades granted Orpheus's heartfelt wish and allowed Eurydice to follow her husband out of the land of the dead. But he warned Orpheus not to look back to see if she was behind him. Unfortunately Orpheus did look back. He wanted to be sure that she was indeed following him. But when he turned around, Eurydice faded into a **shade** or spirit, and Orpheus never saw her again.

Beauty and the Beast

Another well-known tale is that of Psyche, a beautiful young woman who was sent to Hades on an errand for her mother-in-law. Psyche was married to Cupid (or Eros), the god of love. His mother was Venus (Aphrodite). Venus was very jealous of Psyche's great beauty. Out of spite, she gave Psyche several difficult errands or tasks to prove to Cupid that his young wife was not deserving of his love. But Psyche completed each task, including sorting thousands of tiny seeds into piles before nightfall. Finally Venus ordered Psyche to go to the netherworld and bring back Queen Persephone's makeup box.

With great fear and trembling, Psyche made her descent into Hades. She took two coins for Charon, the ferryman, and six honey cakes for Cerberus. Psyche trembled when she heard the hellhound's loud barking. But when Cerberus saw her, he was struck dumb by her loveliness. Instead of lunging at her, he whimpered and wagged his tail. Some versions of the tale say that Charon was so awestruck by Psyche's beauty that he rowed her across the River Styx for free.

Psyche gained entrance to the underworld by charming both Cerberus and the ferryman Charon with her beauty.

Psyche entered the gates of Hades without being harmed, and with Queen Persephone's permission, she took the makeup box to Venus.

A Drugged Doggy Treat

Cerberus appears in other tales, too. The *Aeneid* is an epic poem by Virgil, a classical Roman poet. He lived more than 2,000 years ago. His tale is named after a Trojan hero named Aeneas, who escapes the burning city of Troy after it is attacked and destroyed by the Greeks. Virgil gives an account of the hero's adventures, including his desperate journey into Hades to seek his dead father's advice. Aeneas is

guided on this dangerous journey into the underworld by the Sibyl of Cumae, a powerful priestess of the god Apollo. She warns him to be brave, as the journey will require all the courage he is capable of gathering. The Sibyl takes along some bread soaked with honey for Cerberus. Some stories say they were honey cakes like the ones Psyche used. The treats were drugged with a sedative to make the watchdog fall asleep. Virgil describes the encounter like this:

> Grim Cerberus, who soon began to rear
> His crested snakes, and armed his bristling hair.
> The prudent Sibyl had before prepared
> A sop, in honey steeped, to charm the guard;
> Which, mixed with powerful drugs, she cast before
> His greedy grinning jaws, just op'd to roar.
> With three enormous mouths he gapes; and straight,
> With hunger pressed, devours the pleasing bait.
> Long draughts of sleep his monstrous limbs enslave;
> He reels, and, falling, fills the spacious cave.
> The keeper charmed, the chief without delay
> Passed on, and took the irremeable way.

CHAPTER 3

TRACKING THE HELLHOUNDS

Terrifying hellhounds like Cerberus and Orthus are not unique to Greek and Roman mythology. Many cultures around the world also have ancient tales of fierce canine creatures who guard the entrance to the underworld. Some scholars say that ideas for these mythical creatures were inspired by actual dogs seen feasting on the bodies of fallen warriors and scavenging the dead on battlefields. Interestingly enough, many of the mythical dogs from other cultures are said to be black with more than one head—just like Cerberus. In several of the stories, the spirits must cross a large body of water to get to the dwelling of the dead.

The Huron and Iroquois tribes of North America once told grim tales of dead souls fighting ferocious

Chinese Foo Dog statues have the body of a dog and the head of a lion.

Cerberus

attack dogs as they crossed over a bridge spanning a river into the afterlife. The ancient Chinese Foo Dogs have the appearance of a large dog with a lion's head–rather like the middle head of Cerberus. Foo Dogs are sacred in the Buddhist religion. According to tradition they guarded temple gates, tombs, and other sacred buildings and kept away the evil spirits and other unwanted intruders. The Shisa are also part dog and part lion. They are traditional Ryukyuan decorations on the island of Okinawa, Japan. These guard dogs are usually displayed in pairs. According to tradition one has its mouth open to allow the good spirits to come in. The other has its mouth closed to keep the bad spirits out.

DOGS OF DEATH AND DECAY

Surma is a monster in Finnish mythology very much like Cerberus. He is a huge, violent dog with flaring nostrils and a terrible, snakelike tail. His jaws of steel are always open, ready to devour his victim with supernatural speed. His fangs are like sharp swords. One glance from Surma's angry eyes can turn a helpless victim to stone. His name means "to kill."

Surma is the guardian of Tuonela, the ancient Finnish underworld. Long ago the Finns buried a club with their dead so they could beat off Surma's savage attacks. This beast belongs to Tuoni and Tuonetar, the rulers of the land of the dead, and their four dwarfish daughters: Loviatar, Kipu-Tytto,

Kivutar, and Vammatar. When not patrolling the borders of Tuonela, Surma can be found in Kalma's stench-filled house. Kalma is the goddess of death and decay, who occasionally leaves her underworld home to haunt Finnish graveyards.

In Norse mythology Garm is the watchdog of the house of the dead. This monstrous, **slavering** canine is frequently depicted with more than one head. He has four eyes on each head. His snarling mouth and heaving chest drip with the blood of his slain victims. Like Cerberus, the howling Garm is chained to the entrance of Helheim—the house of hell. In the epic tales of Norway, it is said that Tyr, the god of war, killed Garm. The battle was so fierce that in the end, Tyr died too from the savage bites inflicted by the beast.

Scavengers and Devil Dogs

In ancient Persia, now called Iran, corpses were actually left for the dogs to dispose of. Because the dogs ate **carrion**, they were considered unclean. Persians went out of their way to avoid dogs, believing the evil spirits that haunted the dead bodies often possessed them.

One of the oldest tales of such devil dogs is a Hindu myth from India. The two dogs of Yama were said to have nasty tempers. Their main task was to prevent souls from entering a place called Bliss. One dog was black and the other spotted. Both had four eyes and wide, flaring nostrils. Their

The Hindu god Yama supposedly had two bad-tempered dogs who kept souls from entering a place called Bliss.

master was Yama, king of the netherworld and judge of the dead. Yama had green skin and red clothing. He carried a club in one hand and a hangman's noose in the other. Like his vicious dogs, he enjoyed tormenting the wicked.

Anubis, God of Death

Perhaps the most well-known canine creature associated with the dead is Anubis. In Egyptian mythology Anubis is sometimes shown as a **jackal** and sometimes as a man with the head of a black dog. In ancient Egypt it was common to see wild jackals lurking around tombs and gravesites. Some scholars believe that Egyptians built elaborate tombs to protect their dead from being scavenged by jackals and other wild beasts.

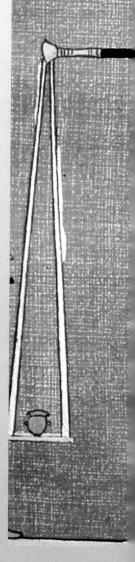

According to legend Anubis guarded the tombs of the dead. He was also worshipped as a god of death. His duties were many. He watched over the mummification process to be sure that all was done properly. After leading souls into the underworld, Anubis placed their hearts on the scales of Justice. He weighed these organs during the Judging of the Heart ceremony. Anubis fed those who were declared to be wicked to Ammit, a fierce demon with

Anubis was an Egyptian god sometimes shown with the head of a dog and the body of a man. He weighed the hearts of the dead on the scales of Justice, while the crocodile-headed monster Ammit waited to eat those who were found to be wicked.

the head of a crocodile. Prayers to Anubis have been found carved on ancient tombs in Egypt, including those of the pharaohs, such as King Tutankhamen.

BLACK DOG SIGHTINGS

Although it is hard to believe, there are some people today who say they have seen large, supernatural canines. In most cases, the dog is huge—the size of a calf. It is black with fierce, glowing eyes and can vanish into thin air. Usually these sightings take place at a crossroads. These black dogs are often seen as **omens** of death and are believed to be connected in some way to the underworld.

While many doubt that there are supernatural black dogs terrorizing the countryside, others swear they have seen them and shudder to recall the incidents. Researchers of black dog lore collect eyewitness accounts, which sound like ghost stories or UFO encounters. Sightings have taken place around the world but mostly in Great Britain and the southern United States.

In October 1969 a British driver reported a large black dog the size of a Great Dane in the mid-

Cerberus

Some people claim to have seen large, supernatural black dogs with glowing eyes.

dle of the road. Before he could swerve out of the way, the driver's car "passed through the animal, which then disappeared."[1] In 1972 a member of the British Coast Guard reported a large black hound running on the beach at Great Yarmouth. "Then it stopped, as if looking for someone. As I watched, it vanished before my eyes."[2]

Are the black dogs real? If so, where do they come from and how do they disappear so quickly? Some say that black dog encounters are an example of folktales and superstitions being passed down through the generations. People believe such tales simply because others in their families do. Some insist that those who report seeing black dogs only imagined that they saw them. Others insist the black dog sightings are just pranks. Researchers are trying to find logical explanations for these sightings.

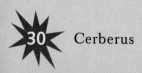

CHAPTER 4

CERBERUS LIVES!

Through the years the monstrous, three-headed canine has continued to fascinate artists and illustrators. Cerberus has been depicted on vases, frescoes, and mosaics. He has been immortalized in bronze and marble statues. Cerberus is pictured on postage stamps from Greece, Monaco, and the Marshall Islands.

Many classical painters have captured the battle between Hercules and Cerberus on canvas. Their work is on display around the world in famous galleries and museums, such as the Louvre in Paris, France. In his bold watercolor *Psyche and Cerberus*, French painter Edmund Dulac (1882–1953) portrayed the encounter between Cupid's beautiful wife and the vicious hellhound. Boris Vallejo's

1988 oil painting, *Hercules and Cerberus*, shows the hero subduing the monster with his bare hands. Modern fantasy illustrators, such as Joseph J. Calkins and Mike Dubisch, also find Cerberus an intriguing subject today.

CERBERUS IN LITERATURE

In *The Divine Comedy*, often considered the greatest literary work in the Italian language, the poet Dante describes Cerberus as a "cruel monster, fierce and strange." The poem tells of the author's imaginary journey to the three realms of the dead. There he sees terrible Cerberus standing guard over **gluttons** in the third circle of hell. Here the ground is soggy from constant rain and hail and snow. It stinks of mildew. The Roman poet Virgil throws the barking beast a sop and accompanies Dante on the remainder of his fantastic journey.

One of Sir Arthur Conan Doyle's best-selling mystery novels features a demonic hound, similar in many ways to Cerberus. In *The Hound of the Baskervilles*, Sherlock Holmes and Dr. Watson visit the Baskerville estate on the Devonshire moors, where they learn about the legend of the Hound of the Baskervilles. This murderous, glow-in-the-dark beast supposedly killed Sir Hugo Baskerville in the 18th century and has haunted every male in the Baskerville family for over 100 years. Holmes suspects that a villain has brought the hellhound myth to life by training a huge, vicious dog to attack men

The Sherlock Holmes story The Hound of the Baskervilles *features the famous detective investigating the legend of a large, ghostly black dog who haunts the male members of the Baskerville family.*

in the Baskerville family, and he sets out to discover the killer before his friend Sir Henry becomes the next victim.

J.K. Rowling also introduces a giant three-headed canine in her novel *Harry Potter and the Sorcerer's Stone*. She calls him Fluffy. Like Cerberus, he can be lulled to sleep by music. Fluffy belongs to Rubeus Hagrid and guards a trapdoor that leads to an underground chamber where the sought-after Sorcerer's Stone is hidden.

CERBERUS IN MOVIES AND ON TELEVISION

The ferocious canine creature has appeared in several science-fiction and fantasy films. In 2005 *Cerberus*, starring Greg Evigan and Brent Florence, was shown on the Sci Fi Movie Channel. When mercenaries steal Attila the Hun's magical sword, Cerberus, in all his rage and fury, is unleashed upon the modern-day world.

The canine with the jaws of steel also appeared in *Hercules in the Underworld* (1994), the fourth made-for-TV movie in the series *Hercules: The Legendary*

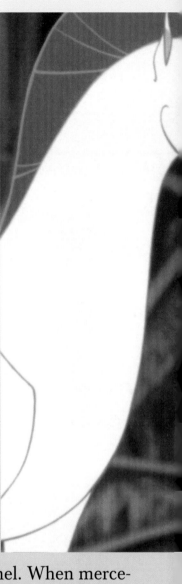

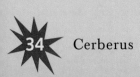

Cerberus appeared as a character in the 1997 Disney animated movie Hercules.

Journeys, starring Kevin Sorbo as the heroic slayer of monsters. In this episode Hercules comes to the rescue of villagers who have fallen into a deep crack in the earth that leads to the underworld realm. At the

Cerberus Lives!

entrance Hercules finds only the hellhound's collar. Hades makes a deal with Hercules: If the strong man can recapture Cerberus, then he can take his wife, Deianeira, back to Earth with him. Hercules finds the beast and defeats him in a ferocious battle. As soon as he chains the monster to the entrance of the underworld, the hole closes over and Hercules returns to the village with his long-lost wife.

Cerberus is one of the many monsters featured in the 1997 Disney animated film *Hercules.* The voice of actor Tate Donovan is used for Hercules. The voice of James Woods is used for Hades, god of the underworld and the villain in the movie.

TOYS, GAMES, AND COMICS

Cerberus and other hellhounds are popular creatures in comic books and video games. Papo, a French company, makes a high-quality plastic Cerberus toy. The beast is black with three snarling heads. In the video role-playing game Final Fantasy VII: Dirge of Cerberus, the popular character Vincent Valentine has a triple-barrel revolver named Cerberus. Collectors can buy a replica of the weapon, which is approximately 6 inches (15cm) long. It has detailing of the dogs' heads on each side of the barrel. It has opening and spinning cylinders, a triple-hammer that can be cocked, and a working trigger.

Cerberus became a Marvel Comics hero in July 1966. Like all immortals he has superhuman

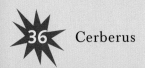

strength. In his original bloodthirsty canine form, he has multiple heads with poisonous fangs. Cerberus can also shape-shift into human form. He carries a powerful war hammer and wears a helmet that fires blasts of energy. He has the supernatural ability to transform any ordinary object into a deadly weapon. The Cerberus superhero character has appeared in issues of *Superman* and *Aquaman*, too.

THE HELLHOUND'S NAMESAKES

According to myth, Cerberus was never killed. He was a brutally efficient and reliable watchdog. Of all the monstrous offspring of Typhon and Echidna, Cerberus alone survived. His legend lives on in a variety of ways and through some strange namesakes. For instance, there is a water snake common in the marshy mangrove habitat and mudflats of Southeast Asia that bears the name Cerberus, or "dog-faced water snake." It feeds mainly on fish and crabs. It moves swiftly through the water pursuing its prey. It kills its victims with a mild venom that drips down the grooves in its fangs. The snake gives off a foul smell and may bite when it is cornered by an enemy.

Astronomers have named a large dark spot on the planet Mars after the legendary hellhound. This feature is located on the southeastern edge of the large Elysium Mons volcanic area. There is also an asteroid named "1865 Cerberus," which was discovered in 1971 by the famous Czechoslovakian

Astronomers named a large dark spot on the planet Mars after Cerberus.

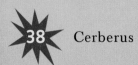

Cerberus

astronomer Lubos Kohoutek. Mount Cerberus in the state of Alaska is 3,491 feet (1,064m) above sea level. It is located in the Valley of Ten Thousand Smokes in Katmai National Park.

The British built a turreted warship and named it the HMVS *Cerberus*. It was launched in 1868 to defend the colony of Victoria in Australia and was the first major British warship to be entirely steam powered.

In 1942 during World War II the Nazis launched Operation Cerberus. Adolf Hitler became concerned that the British were planning to attack his troops in Norway. He ordered the German fleet, led by three heavily armed warships, to move north to the Norwegian Sea channels. After consulting a map, Hitler then suggested they travel north through the English Channel–right under the noses of the British forces and straight through their naval defense lines. When his stunned admirals protested, "Hitler coldly replied that if the big ships could be of no use, then they must be scrapped and their guns and armor sent to reinforce the Norwegian coastal defenses."[3]

Despite losses on both sides and many tense moments, Operation Cerberus–later called the Great Channel Dash–was a military success. German admiral Otto Ciliax later said, "It had been a day that will probably go down as one of the most daring in the naval history of this war."[4]

Even today many security or safety-related companies use the name, such as Cerberus Pyrotronics. This company sells fire alarm parts and other fire safety products. The Cerberus FTP server provides computer security and uses a three-headed dog in its **logo**.

For centuries Cerberus and other canine creatures like him have captured the imagination of people around the world. It continues to do so in art, movies, and advertising. But beware! This dog's bite *is* worse than its bark!

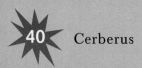

NOTES

CHAPTER 3: TRACKING THE HELLHOUNDS

1. Quoted in Jerome Clark, *Unexplained!* Detroit: Visible Ink, 1999, pp. 400–401.
2. Quoted in Clark, *Unexplained!*, pp. 400–401.

CHAPTER 4: CERBERUS LIVES!

3. Quoted in George Constable, ed., *War on the High Seas.* Alexandria, VA: Time-Life, 1990, p. 114.
4. Quoted in Constable, *War on the High Seas*, p. 120.

GLOSSARY

canine: An animal of the Canidae family, such as dogs, wolves, coyotes, and jackals.

carrion: Dead and rotting bodies of animals or humans, unfit for human food.

gluttons: People who like to eat and drink too much.

Hades: Dwelling place of the dead, named after the Greek god of the underworld, Hades, who is called Pluto in Roman mythology.

jackal: A nocturnal canine mammal related to a dog.

logo: A sign, name, or trademark often used in advertising.

lyre: A small harp used by ancient Greek musicians.

mortals: Of or relating to humankind.

netherworld: The world of the dead.

omens: Signs or occurrences that foretell good or evil.

sedative: A drug used to calm people down or help them go to sleep.

shade: In Greek mythology, the formless body or spirit of a dead person.

slavering: Drooling or slobbering.

For Further Exploration

Books

Robert Burleigh, *Hercules.* Bel Air, CA: Silver Whistle, 1999. This picture book offers a suspenseful retelling of Hercules' final labor, to capture the Hound of Hades.

Jerome Clark, *Unexplained!* Detroit, MI: Visible Ink, 1999. This fascinating reference book compiles the strange and unexplained sightings of savage black dogs, the Loch Ness monster, and other cryptozoological creatures.

Nancy Hathaway, *The Friendly Guide to Mythology: A Mortal's Companion to the Fantastical Realm of Gods, Goddesses, Monsters, Heroes.* New York, NY: Penguin, 2003. This large collection of world myths, including Greek and Roman, contains sidebars, a glossary, and plenty of illustrations.

Ellen Switzer, *Greek Myths: Gods, Heroes and Monsters.* New York, NY: Atheneum, 1988. This is a catalog of tales about the royal family of the Greek gods and goddesses, from Apollo to Zeus.

Web Sites

The Creatures Library (http://reference.howstuff works.com/greek-roman-creatures-encyclopedia-channel.html). Find lots of information here on creatures from Greek and Roman mythology.

Encyclopedia Mythica (www.pantheon.org). Read more than 7,000 articles about heroes and monsters in Greek, Roman, and Norse mythology, including Cerberus, Hercules, and Orthus.

Mythological Monsters (www.monsters.monstrous.com). This site contains lots of information on Cerberus, his parents, Typhon and Echidna, and all their monstrous offspring.

Perseus Digital Library (www.perseus.tufts.edu/Herakles/cerberus.html). This site offers detailed accounts of the Twelve Labors of Hercules, including the slaying of Orthus and the capture of Cerberus.

INDEX

Picture Credits

About the Author

Shirley-Raye Redmond is the author of several non-fiction books for children, including *Mermaids, The Alamo,* and *Patriots in Petticoats: Heroines of the American Revolution.* Redmond lives in New Mexico.